MW00340350

Quinn Conyers

Foreword by Brian J. Olds

SPEAK
BLACK
WOMAN

. . . .

HOW WOMEN IN BUSINESS CAN
PROFIT FROM PUBLIC SPEAKING

Cover design by Marshall Fox
Book interior design by Davon Christian Brown

First Paperback Edition, May 2021

Dedication

This book is dedicated to my mom and Aunt Stine, who directly and indirectly showed me the importance of having a voice as a young black girl growing up in Lancaster, PA. It is through both of you I've learned so many public and private lessons that stick with me when it comes to having, using, and leveraging my voice. My voice was shaped, molded, and sculpted by the life lessons you consciously and unconsciously instilled in me, and because of that, I am forever grateful for the roles you played in my life.

To my husband Isa, you have reminded me from day one that I have ALWAYS been a speaker, especially when I doubted my voice and committed to only being an entrepreneur. When I felt the world didn't want to hear what I had to say, you always listened, encouraged, and had those powerful 1-liners that would stick with me for weeks and months after our conversations. You have been a constant force in reminding me of who I am as an 'Abdul-Raheem' and how quitting and giving up is not a part of our DNA. I love you for having my back and affirming my voice since the day we met.

Acknowledgements

To Tiffany Bethea, I still chuckle as you always remind me that you have your notes from my Power Speaker workshop I hosted back in 2012. It's because of you I reactivated my voice years after being frustrated not making a profit from speaking. It was a simple conversation with your powerful words, "Quinn, you are not good at speaking, you are anointed to speak," that resurrected the fire in me to grab that mic one more time, and I have never looked back. Thank you for believing in me when I doubted myself and showing me the holes in my speaking business that are now filled due to your coaching, training, and mentorship. God used you to speak to me, and for that, I am forever grateful for your friendship and sisterhood.

To Chenire Harrell-Carter, you have been my champion and cheerleader since the day we served as co-speakers on a Heal a Woman to Heal a Nation conference call. I appreciate how you have 'served' me in my speaking and entrepreneurial journey. You have been a profit partner, idea bouncer-offer, and ledge talker offer since the day we met. Your DNA is all over my voice, and I'm grateful for your friendship.

CONTENTS

FOREWORD

Prepare to have your glass shattered!

Have you ever had a moment in your life when your beliefs were shattered into a thousand pieces, like a glass plate?

When I first heard Quinn speak in the Fall of 2008, I thought I was doing something as a speaker. Having just joined a Toastmasters club at Morgan State University a year prior, I felt like I was already the top speaker on campus. I would soon find out what a powerful speaker really was.

By the time I encountered Quinn, she was no stranger to the stage. She was a professor of communications at Coppin State University. She had earned a master's in mass communication from Howard University. On top of all that, Quinn had even already created her own public speaking company called Speak2Society.

Of course, my friend Dipo Adesina and I did not know any of this when we casually invited Quinn to be a guest speaker at our Toastmasters club. As she confidently took the stage that evening and powerfully ripped into her presentation, here's an insider's window into what was happening in my mind within the first minute of her speech:

- 5 Seconds: "Oh wow! This is a different kind of speech..."
- 15 Second: "What is actually happening right now?"
- 30 Seconds: "Yo! Who is this?
- 60 Seconds: "Okay... I'm not a speaker... SHE is a speaker..."

Fast forward over a decade later, I am still absolutely blown away anytime Quinn Conyers graces any stage, virtual or live. She has an undeniable aurora that all top athletes, performers, and professionals at the highest level exude when operating in their zone of genius. However, even with all those accolades, that is not the reason I am MOST excited that you are reading this book.

You see, Quinn could easily take her talents and

focus on building her own platform, but she has never been that way. She has crafted life-changing programs like "Power at the Podium." She has created valuable communities like "Speak Black Woman." And now, with this book, it is clear that Quinn is on a lifelong journey to empower and equip black women in business who are also passionate about making a PROFIT from public speaking.

By reading this book, you are unlocking instant access to a culmination of well over two decades of experience, investment and, refinement in public speaking. Quinn has done it so that you can benefit from her expertise, but...you MUST still do the work. What you will not find in these pages are get-rich-quick schemes, unproven rhetoric, or empty promises.

Every year, thousands of new people claim that they want to become speakers, but very few can commit to something as simple as purchasing a book like this to invest in their success. Congratulations to you! If you are reading these words, you have already boldly separated yourself from the 98% who claim that they want more money, time, flexibility, and impact from public speaking.

I know Quinn. I trust Quinn. I believe in Quinn. Her presence and thought leadership has consistently shaped the direction of Black Speakers Network from the very beginning. She is a living legend in the speaking industry as evidenced by the thousands of people she continues to impact.

Don't just read this book; anyone can do that. Instead, I challenge you to finish it, then internalize it, and then implement it. Quinn and I will know within 24 to 48 months if you accepted this challenge because, by that point, you will be the one on stage with people in the audience wondering… "yo! who is this"?

Prepare to have your glass shattered!

Brian J. Olds
President & Founder
Black Speakers Network

To black women in business who are ready to use their voice to profit from public speaking and those who have been their cheerleaders. It's time to raise your voice.

Love Quinn

Who is this book for?

In 2014 I lost my voice in front of 100 people. At the time, I was a successful handbag vendor and had begun hosting workshops teaching other entrepreneurs how to get paid selling their products at events. I rented space in a venue called Signature Blue Events in Landover, Maryland, and sent out as many invitations as possible. One hundred seventy people RSVP'd, but only one hundred people showed up. I secured three vendors to set up their merchandise tables, invested in a videographer, and a photographer. I even convinced eight of my good girlfriends to serve as volunteers. Yet, when I made an offer to work with me no one enrolled in my coaching program. As a result, I lost my voice and decided to focus on selling bags and retire my hopes and dreams of being a speaker.

Over the next four hours I shared all of my secrets on being a successful seller while vending at events. I showed the entrepreneurs how to set up their vending tables, greet customers, affirm the sale, and increase their chances of having those customers buy from them online. At the end of the presentation, I offered them the opportunity to work with me in "Victorious Vendor", a six-week coaching program for "only $397." I expected half of the attendees to jump up from their seats, race to the back of the room, and enroll. But, the opposite happened. No one moved, and no one registered. I was devastated. I felt as if I had poured out my heart and soul to the love of my life, and he told me the "feeling wasn't mutual," or he just "wanted to be friends." Feeling down and broken, I convinced myself that making money while speaking on my own platform wasn't possible for me. So, I put my head down, gave up on public speaking, and put all my effort and energy into being the Purse Paparazzi Chief Fashion Officer. And like that, the public speaker, in me, was silenced for the next three years.

This experience, and so many others, are why I wrote this book is for black women with service-based businesses. Those who have tried and failed to consistently make money selling their products, program, or services after they speak. Whether you are a financial services expert, a business coach, or even an aspiring speaker, if you are looking for strategies to use your voice for your business and optimize the time spent finding and enrolling clients or customers, this book is for you!

If you are an entrepreneur who is already hosting workshops and seminars or other types of events, and you find yourself offering your services, yet, no one is hiring your services, then stick with me, we are going to change this trajectory. And for my black businesswomen who are looking to penetrate the speaking business and become a non-traditional, paid speaker. This book is for you too.

I often hear how speakers struggle as they seek ways to monetize their speaking business. I also hear how entrepreneurs are not maximizing their voice to secure clients for their business. It does not mean that these speakers don't have a dynamic message or impactful services; speaking is a craft that requires a tailored and strategic approach to deliver a powerful presentation that gets you paid. Knowing how to convey who you are, what you do, and the value of the services you offer, clearly and concisely, takes artful planning and preparation. When your messages are clear, tailored, and robust, you will begin to stand out, and speaking will become a consistent stream of income for you.

When speaking, you want your audience to touch, taste, feel, smell, and hear every single word that comes out of your mouth. Here is where the value of what you say amplifies what you offer.

If you haven't figured out the benefits that public

speaking can add to your business, this is a must-read for you. I will teach you some key strategies that will transform your life and legacy as a black woman in business. We are about to embark on a journey that will take your public speaking efforts to another level, a level that will, in turn, elevate your businesses.

I'm excited that you picked up this book. No more being tired of wasting time speaking and walking away feeling undervalued or, worse, not converting the audience into paying clients. Not only will you learn key strategies on how to enhance your public speaking platform, but I will also teach you how to use your voice and message to reach your broader audience, leveraging the one-on-many model. You have the tools to take your life, sanity, and time back, giving you the luxury of being present for your family while still being a successful CEO and speaker.

Speak Black Woman! You are on a mission to leverage the power of your voice to build your business, get hired by more clients, and get more strategic, confident, and clear when presenting your message and the value of your services. So, if you love the idea of genuinely using your voice, enhancing your communication skills to lead you to increased client conversion, this book has your name written all over it, and I'm glad that it's finally in your hands.

2

Speak Black Woman

Unmute the voice of the black woman!

"Don't speak unless spoken to" and "Be seen and not heard" are both powerful examples of the ways black women have been silenced since childhood. The damage doesn't stop there; it carries well into adulthood. Passionate, ambitious, and vocal black women have been stereotyped as aggressive, or worst, "the angry black woman."

The black woman's voice has been disrespected for way too long! I am so excited to honor, glorify, validate, confirm, and affirm the black woman's voice. Over time and as I worked with my customers and clients, I became increasingly aware that I had been serving the black woman all along and had not necessarily been conscious or intentional about it. I now, consciously, serve black women by showing them how to elevate and leverage their voice in every aspect of their business.

To ensure my effectiveness in giving black women back their voices, I realized a mental makeover and a mind-shifting had to occur. When given opportunities to express ourselves, we often find it difficult. Not because we are unable to exercise our voice's power, but because we have been postured to feel uncomfortable instead of empowered when we want to speak up. The result is, we end up not using or exercising our voice in the impactful and meaningful ways that we should. It's no wonder that when we find ourselves in an environment that encourages us to speak up and to be heard, we have a tough time doing so because we don't want to seem like we're "bragging" or "boasting," or like we are a "know-it-all." This applies in and out of business. And is especially true for black women.

I believe that public speaking is a critical skill that every woman, especially black women in business, needs to master. However, many of us have been 'muted' in our roles in Corporate America or other business spaces. These experiences do more to our mindset around public speaking than we may realize. We end up carrying this mindset into our businesses and entrepreneurial endeavors, and unfortunately, it can lead to our business' demise.

While black women are celebrated as the fastest-growing group of entrepreneurs, we are also failing the fastest and employing the least number of people. We are not failing because we don't have potentially great businesses. We are failing because we are unable to verbalize the value of our products or services. Here is where the mindset shift needs to occur, and we have to be bold, open, and transparent enough to talk about it because no one else is.

I've decided to use my voice and contribute to leading the charge in transforming black women in business to articulate their awesomeness and verbalize their value. I want women to maximize and monetize all speaking opportunities on behalf of their business. I also want them to leverage their voice as a lead generation tool and for funding their businesses. You can also use public speaking as a revenue-generating marketing strategy. There is a sense of liberation and power that comes when we are unmuted.

Exciting, right? However, before we jump into how you can leverage your voice and maximize every speaking opportunity you get, it's essential to understand the mind and attitude shift that needs to take place. You won't go to bed one night, wake up the next morning, and all the years of conditioning are gone. Some work needs to be done. You must shed all the years of suppression, muting, and muzzling of your voice. Once this happens, real transformation will begin.

The women who I genuinely serve are women who

have run the Corporate America rat race and have decided that it's time to use the power of their voices in their businesses. These women may or may not realize that their voices have been silenced. I am here to show you how to be a vocal advocate for your awesomeness.

These highly educated women stepped into the workforce extremely excited. They took on leadership roles or responsibilities, shared their visions, ideas, and gifts. They freely gave of their time and sacrificed in ways they eventually came to regret. Yet, somewhere along the way, their voices were muted. It may have been blatant and direct, although frequently, it was indirect, subliminal, and inferred. You know the signs and the cues. They started with irritated looks in meetings when we shared a great idea, of course, because we thought of it first. Or when we advocate or passionately express ourselves and subsequently are told that we are "aggressive" or implied to be "the angry black woman." And the familiar blatant stealing of our ideas by anyone who feels they are privileged to them. These and many other reasons are why amazingly talented black women decide to start their businesses. This is why I have made it my duty to give them back the power of their voices!

Once you decide to walk away from the Corporate America rat race, you begin the process of shedding the conditioning you faced for so long. This brave step deserves to be celebrated and acknowledged. Then the real transformation begins.

Funding, sponsorships, business partners, customers, clients, consultants, and even employees are all some of the elements you'll need to consider.

Most of you have hired business coaches, sought mentors, and pursued memberships or subscriptions to groups or organizations that promise strategic networking opportunities. You may have attended conferences and webinars or even enrolled in entrepreneurship courses to bring your skills, talents, and knowledge to the people you will now serve. The problem is that many of these programs don't address the mental makeover you women need. You have poured your passion, energy, and ambition into your former environments and were handcuffed, diminished, and silenced. Therefore, your greatness, fire, power, strength, purpose, and execution now need to be resurrected to succeed in your businesses.

So, to support you amazing women in your entrepreneurial endeavors and to give you back your voice, *Speak Black Woman* will be a go-to resource to teach you how to use the power of your voice to profit from public speaking.

Entrepreneurs
Who Speak

I have found that black women have a variety of reasons for entering the world of entrepreneurship. In most cases, these reasons are very similar. Some are second and third-generation entrepreneurs and have witnessed their parents or other family members' success or failures in their businesses. Others have been influenced and inspired by seeing their friends launch businesses. At the same time, many have felt an overwhelming dissatisfaction in their jobs and have decided to apply their skills and knowledge to something more fulfilling, self-started, and rewarding. Whatever the reason, black women have realized the value, potential, and control of being their 'own' boss.

They begin to take steps to start and elevate their businesses. They seek to build a solid foundation by seeking out coaches and experts who can help them dial in on their vision. Business kicks off and they set off on their journeys. As they navigate the entrepreneurial terrain, something happens that they are not ready for or even expecting. They are solicited and sought out for speaking opportunities. Others start to see the value and impact of their mission and want to hear more from them. Sounds great, right? Well, not so much, at least not initially, for the entrepreneur who has now become a public speaker, by 'accident.' They have barely gotten their feet wet as an entrepreneur, yet, they are thrust into the speaking realm, and they are not sure how to handle it.

Ladies, what I want you to take away from this chapter, is to understand the power, influence, and impact your voice can have in making you money. Speaking should be a part of your business and viewed as a stream of income. Speaking should also be considered as part of your marketing strategy and leveraged as a lead generation tool for your business.

I want to dive into three things that every black female entrepreneur should know about speaking and its elevation on your entrepreneurial journey.

The first thing is, as an entrepreneur, you need to think more entrepreneurial about speaking. Often, entrepreneurs are excited, honored, and humbled when invited to speak and share their passion. However, they show up, speak life into the audience, yet still leave empty-handed, with no new leads or clients, no publicity, no footage of themselves speaking, and no paycheck. They have not capitalized or monetized on the opportunity. This is the wrong way to go about your speaking business, and yes, speaking is now a part of your business. So, I'm going to teach you how to treat it as such.

Next, I want you to consider a cost-benefit analysis. Yes, because you should be thinking about speaking as a part of your business, you need to be sure that you do not end up in the "red" (negative income or loss) sort of speak. This doesn't always equate to a dollar-for-dollar scenario. It can be a dollar-for-access or dollar-for-value situation. The point here is that you want to be sure that you are walking away with something that adds to your bottom line, now or in the future. If you are getting paid upfront or an honorarium to speak, that is undoubtedly a great thing. Be sure that payment covers any expenses you may incur, like travel, as an example. If you are not receiving any upfront payment, here is where the real cost-benefit analysis comes into consideration. What value are you receiving for your time?

You want to make sure that you will be allowed an opportunity, and be sure it's a tangible one, not indirect or subliminal, to walk away with value-add things. Examples are access to their email list of all the people who register to attend the event. This way, you can add them to your email campaign, and they become part of your funnel. Video footage and action photos of you speaking at the event are valuable as you build your speaking portfolio. And very important, be sure they will allow you to offer your services after your speech. Take the answers to these requests and assess their value for your business and the potential cost you may incur to attend the event; travel, childcare, hotel accommodations, etc. If you determine that the benefits outweigh the cost, then it's a GO for you. Otherwise, it should be a NO for you.

It's great to feel honored by an opportunity to speak to an audience who needs your message but don't forget, this is also your business, and you must always treat it that way.

The third thing you must consider as part of your speaking business is to leverage every opportunity for future marketing, promotion, publicity, and social proof. Testimonials from the people who attended the event, those who heard you speak go a long way. They are as crucial as "word of mouth." Having someone who has witnessed your greatness give a raving testimonial is undoubtedly worth the effort of asking for it. These testimonials may be used in your email campaign, social media marketing, and on your website, to name a few ways you can leverage them. Whatever you do, gather as many recorded and or written testimonials as possible whenever you can.

Again, these are three things that can be of great value for your lead generation strategy. As people hear you speak or see the proof of your speaking, they may be prompted to have you speak at their events. Or others may make an instant decision about investing in your services. Therefore, you want to think about how you can have a more entrepreneurial mindset regarding your speaking career.

The Birth of an Entrepreneur

In 2005 I decided to turn down an apprenticeship at the University of South Florida for an opportunity to attend Howard University. Some people thought I was crazy, but I knew that I wanted a cultural experience as part of my college education. I'd just graduated from West Chester University in Pennsylvania, a predominantly white institution of higher education and yearned for diversity. Once I entered Howard University, I instantly knew that my education had really just begun. I was ready to embrace a historically black university experience. It was one of the best decisions I ever made.

From the moment I stepped on campus, I was greeted with "black girl magic," strength, and wisdom from students who wanted to navigate this world. And the best part, they looked like me. Students were eager to get to class and learn what they could use and apply to their lives, careers, and businesses. It was a magical experience.

I vividly recall my first day of class. The moment we walked in, the Professor immediately instilled in us the standard by which a student at Howard University lived. Everything was addressed, from how we were expected to dress, to how we were expected to conduct our behavior. It was clear that the way we showed up and represented ourselves for class would become how we showed up and presented ourselves to the world. This was a completely different approach to learning than what I was accustomed to at West Chester University. However, it deeply resonated with me and was a culture into which I smoothly transitioned.

One of my favorite memories attending Howard University was when I decided to study mass communication and media studies. An administrator in the Department of the School of Communication, also known as the school of C, informed me that I had to select a concentration. The intent of determining a concentration was to allow us to fully master a chosen area. While most of my classmates chose journalism or public relations, I decided to study entrepreneurship, a concentration in the School of Business. I was required to obtain special permission from both schools' deans to participate in classes across both disciplines. This was the beginning of my entrepreneurial journey.

My first class was Intro to Entrepreneurship, taught by Dr. Charles Murphy. I remember him saying, "You guys are navigating this world. You have a lot of education. And I want you to understand that when you graduate from Howard University, if no one offers you a job, you can create your own!" That stuck with me.

Most of my professors were entrepreneurs. Dr. Murphy was the franchise owner of five McDonald food chains in the DC area. I was being taught by people who were not just teaching but were living the entrepreneurial life. That was a real motivation for me. It was also the wake-up call that challenged everything I had been taught about getting out in the world and securing a "good-paying" job. As a member of the Howard University Entrepreneurship Society (HUES), my eyes were further opened to the perspective that I could seek alternative paths that didn't require me to find a job. I had the option to create my own career path by becoming a full-time entrepreneur. That's precisely where I am today.

Many people know about my bag business, Purse Paparazzi. However, Speak2Society was the very first business I founded as a college student. Speak2society was a communications and a public speaking company that trained college students to polish their public speaking skills and explore entrepreneurship as a viable career choice.

As the proud student-president of the company, I earned my first paid speaking engagement and was invited to speak at the Essence Magazine Young Women's Leadership Conference. I also spoke at a conference hosted by the School of Business. Here is where I met two of my mentors Eldridge Allen and Johnetta Hardy, who were part of a new business initiative called the Entrepreneurship Leadership Institute (ELI). Through ELI more light was shed on the world of entrepreneurship. I even had the opportunity to speak alongside Lisa Price, the founder of Carol's Daughter. I was also afforded the chance to be featured in numerous local media outlets. I knew these were all great opportunities, but, little did I know Howard University would birth a businesswoman, speaker, polish my purpose, and confirm my calling.

My entrepreneurial experience is one reason I have chosen to serve entrepreneurs who are also passionate about public speaking.

Going Into Business with my Boyfriend

I launched my second venture when I partnered with my boyfriend to create a bag business called, Purse Paparazzi. (Side bar: I did not know he would later become my husband and father of my children.) We started our custom clutch and handbag business and set out to cater to all women, initially. However, through opportunity and experience we began to focus on black women who were members of sororities or those who attended historically black colleges and universities (HBCU).

Our clutches were wildly popular and profitable, and we began selling at homecoming events and the sorority's regional conferences. We obtained a seller's license with Alpha Kappa Alpha, Delta Sigma Theta, Zeta Phi Beta, and Sigma Gamma Rho, sororities. We also secured several HBCUs, including Howard University and North Carolina A&T.

A valuable key lesson I learned through this experience was super-serving in my niche of Black women; their purchase was also an affirmation that made them feel good.

As the spokesperson and sales "queen" behind Purse Paparazzi, I quickly realized my voice's power and value.

Before I move on, let me briefly share how it all began.

****

At the start of the 2009 New Year, a few friends and I decided to go out to celebrate new beginnings. We ended up at a local lounge. As fate would have it, there was a tall, dark, and handsome guy whose eyes scanned the room and locked with mines. We eyed each other a couple of times before he decided to come over and introduce himself. He was cool and had swag. He immediately wanted to know if I was single. We talked for a bit and exchanged numbers. Our first date was a few days later. We met at his place, and the first thing I noticed when I walked in was a bunch of luggage lined up against his wall. Curious, I asked if he had plans to travel. His response surprised me. He was confident, collected, and said, "No. I sell things." My curiosity had spiked, and I probed a bit more.

I must admit, I was underwhelmed as he shared with me all of the products he sold. However, he pulled out some handbags that immediately stood out to me. I began picking out my favorites and could see the wheels spinning in his eyes. The thing that sealed the deal for my heart was his business acumen. Yes, he liked me. Yes, he wanted to get to know me better. Yes, he even saw a future with me. But he was not going to let me walk away with those bags for free. He quickly totaled up my order and expected payment of $60. A little taken back but with a smile on my face, I paid the man.

As I sported my new handbags, they quickly gained a ton of attention. So, I began referring consumers to my new "friend." When I visited my hometown in Lancaster, Pennsylvania, my friends and family fell in love with my beautiful handbags. I convinced my boyfriend to allow me to take a few bags home and see if I could sell them on my own. One evening, at a family gathering, the trunk of my car became his extended storefront. Within 20-minutes of opening my doors, I sold out of every handbag, purse, and clutch I had. The rush of these quick turn-around transactions sparked my interest in getting a bit deeper into the business, and my boyfriend became my business partner.

We strategized our approach. He was the businessman, and I became the spokeswoman. We began testing out our direct sales business model. We started with what we called "purse parties." We would host events at different women's homes, invite their family and friends, and offer food and drinks to the ambiance. However, we quickly realized we weren't selling as many bags as we thought. It turned out the guests were less interested in buying and more interested in the free food and drinks. So, we had to pivot quickly. We decided to continue with a direct sales model, but we would focus on vending this time. Sales improved slightly, but we had not struck gold just yet. Our current business model was slow in bringing in sales because we were trying to sell to ALL women. Home parties and local vending did not allow us to sell to as many women as possible.

Our big opportunity came when my boyfriend was invited to be a vendor at an event hosted by Alpha Kappa Alpha Sorority, Incorporated (AKA). This experience turned into a rich opportunity to take our hustle and turn it into an official business. The event inspired me to create a pink and green custom "AKA" purse. It proved to be a success, and we were licensed with this sorority and others. Our sales quadrupled, and we entered a new niche market providing custom purses to historically African American sororities.

I was immediately inspired to focus on the black sorority market because of how proud they were of the sisterhood, colors, and love of fashion. I wanted to provide custom clutches so they could carry what they cared about with pride.

So, I researched the requirements to create custom bags for a sorority and the criteria to become a licensed vendor, specifically selling our product to them. We secured our licensure and began selling at events hosted by AKA. This opened up the door for us to obtain licenses to sell custom bags to Delta Sigma Theta Sorority, Inc., Zeta Phi Beta, and Sigma Gamma Rho. We struck our first pot of gold. However, this was only the tip of the iceberg for us. We brainstormed ideas and decided to expand our reach by getting licensed to sell to Historically Black Colleges and Universities (HBCU).

****

Ladies, do not allow anyone to limit your reach or muzzle your authentic voice in your business. We were doing exceptionally well, and our company was growing because we were faithful to our business model and target audience of black women. However, I was frequently questioned about "why was I limiting myself to selling handbags to the sororities and HBCUs?" I couldn't articulate it at the time, but I knew it was more than just the money. I realized how good I felt when I offered our bags to these women.

Their beautiful brown faces would light up, and they would walk taller and feel more confident simply by the clutch they were carrying.

These women noticed something special about me. They often asked, "what do you do?" They sensed I did so much more than just sell handbags and purses. They recognized that there was a power inside of me that I wasn't using. What they did not know was that I had suppressed my voice and had given up on my gift of speaking. I decided to focus on my bag business out of frustration of not making money as a speaker, consistently. Through our encounters they reminded me that I couldn't hide my gift of gab. It shined through as I sold our purses at their events all over the United States.

During our best year of running Purse Paparazzi, we generated over $189,000.00. Although we were making money, I began to feel unfilled, and as I was now a wife and mother of two small boys, I could no longer commit to traveling as a vendor for various events. Furthermore, I had considerably slowed down my public speaking to focus on my bag business. I felt something was missing.

A conversation with my good friend Tiffany Bethea

gave my soul the wake-up call it needed to resurrect my voice. She asked me when I was hosting my next speaking event. I told her I quit, and my focus was selling bags. What she said next left me speechless and put a fire back in my spirit. She said, "Quinn, you are not good at speaking; you are anointed to speak!" I stared at the phone in silence and felt the lion in me awaken because I knew she just broke my silence.

As I look back on this experience and the Purse Paparazzi, it allowed me to find my voice and lead me back to my love for public speaking.

Can I Really
Profit from Public
Speaking?

Why public speaking? That is a question that many entrepreneurs ask. Some small business owners believe that social media, radio, and magazine advertisements are the top ways to spread the word about their businesses. So, why public speaking? While there are a million and one ways to grow, expand, or market a business, I believe that public speaking should be leveraged as an income stream, marketing strategy, and lead generation tool in your business. If you are a black woman in business, I believe your voice is your sales and marketing plan's heartbeat. This is why I am passionate about training black women to be spokespersons for their business, book, or brand.

I genuinely believe that public speaking is the number one skill that every entrepreneur needs to master if they want to be super successful in business. The problem I see, especially with black women, is that we don't know how to verbalize our value or articulate our awesomeness. We are literally leaving money on the table because we are uncomfortable with sales or have a tough time explaining what we do with confidence. We tend to play it safe, shrink or settle for fear of bragging or tooting our own horns too loudly. This must stop. If you want to be successful in business, you have to embrace, leverage, and amplify your voice. Not speaking up will result in leaving money on the table, lack of business confidence, or worse, quitting your business dreams altogether.

Ladies, listen, I need you to understand the power of your voice in your business. I'm sharing this information with you because I love black women in business. I wrote this book because I want to be a part of your growth, development, and transformation. The days of people just buying from you because they like your product or service are over. I want people to buy from you because they can relate to you. They feel connected with your story and your ability to sell what you do with confidence.

I know many black women in business struggling, and it's not because their product or service isn't fantastic. It's because they are only using social media or their website to market and promote their business. That's not enough. Adding public speaking and presenting can scale your business quickly. But, if you remain muted and muzzled, your sales will stagnate, causing unwanted worry or stress.

I personally know the direct impact on my business when I used my voice to sell purses to women. However, I also know how many black women are hurting their business because they haven't leveraged public speaking. So it's time to speak up and make your mouth your #1 marketing strategy for your business.

Public speaking is a great tool and strategy to incorporate into your business. It is often one of those things that organically presents itself as an opportunity for entrepreneurs. However, I believe black women in business need to be more intentional and deliberate about maximizing and monetizing speaking opportunities to sell their products, services, or programs.

I service many black women in business who have become speakers by accident. They often start speaking because someone asked them. However, they don't know how to take full advantage of their speaking opportunities. In some instances some shy away from speaking, while others embrace. Either way, the challenge remains; they don't know how to optimize the opportunities to speak. Nonetheless, these are amazing businesswomen who need guidance, confidence, and strategy to leverage their voice and public speaking in their business. This is where the fun begins for me.

There is a downside of not embracing or polishing

your public speaking skills as an entrepreneur. That downside is, your business will suffer. It hurts my heart whenever I see a fantastic business owner with a superb offering stumble whenever someone asks her about her business or what she does. I've heard some business owners inadvertently and outright downplay their businesses when attempting to explain what they do. I have also witnessed some entrepreneurs speak on stages and leave the audience in a fog of confusion about who they are and what they do because they haven't mastered the art of public speaking.

My passion is to train black women in business to turn conversation into cash to profit from public speaking. I want you to dominate in the world of public speaking so you can make a profit, build, and expand your businesses using a one-on-many model. Speaking offers excellent opportunities to market, promote, and gain publicity for your business. So, if you don't master the art of public speaking, then I guarantee that you are leaving money on the table, and you are likely missing out on great opportunities to promote and publicize your business. And get this...for FREE!

Speaking to your audience or consumers is a necessity if you want to profit from public speaking.

It's also not a one-time event. It can often take somewhere between 7-15 attempts to build likeability and trust from your social media or virtual audience. However, you can give one powerful in-person or virtual presentation and make immediate connections with your audience, resulting in a conversion or sale. My point is that public speaking is a powerful tool in your business and can directly increase your profits. Do not take it lightly.

I am a firm believer that public speaking is crucial for black women in business, and you should, intentionally, make it a part of your business model. If you want to attract new customers and clients, then public speaking is also an excellent way to maximize your impact, influence, and, ultimately, you will profit from publish speaking. Warren Buffett said it so beautifully, "being a great speaker increases your credibility by 50%."

49% Principle

My journey to the 49% principle happened by accident. It started back in college when I was invited to speak at another college, and they agreed to pay me $750. At the time, $750 wasn't anything to turn up my nose at. I was eager and excited to get paid to speak. I had someone drive me from my campus to the location just to give my talk. I was surprised by the idea that people got paid to speak. I immediately knew I wanted to be part of this public speaking life. It was this pivotal moment early in my speaking career that opened my eyes to the possibilities and opportunities to get paid as a speaker.

I was wholly convinced that the only way I could make money as a speaker was to be paid upfront through what the industry calls a "speaker fee" or "honorarium" (the advance payment to a speaker). I was a novice and didn't understand the speaking industry. I didn't realize that there were multiple ways to get paid for speaking, and it didn't necessarily mean getting paid upfront. However, because I fell into the trap of doing it the way I thought every speaker was doing, I *killed* myself trying to get people to pay me to speak. While it worked now and then, there were more times that it just didn't work out, which left me tired, frustrated, and confused. I realized that many event planners wanted recognizable named individuals or celebrities to speak at their events. People who had crowd-drawing potential, and at the time, that wasn't me.

At the time, I was still in college. No one knew who I was, and they certainly weren't trying to pay me to speak. So, I decided to invest in myself and increase my knowledge about the public speaking industry. I attended conferences and read every book I could get my hands on. This is where the light switch went off, and I realized that there were multiple ways to profit from public speaking. Much to my surprise, some of the biggest names in speaking were using these same strategies to make money speaking, while I thought they were all getting paid upfront.

I recall, back in 2013, I had an opportunity to hear Lisa Nichols speak, and I was utterly blown away by how amazing she was on the stage. But what rocked my world was when she admitted that she spoke, "for free all the time." She further shared, "When I broke into the speaking industry, a lot of organizations and companies had money to pay my $25,000 honorarium, but that's not the case anymore because there are more speakers in this space. And the idea of becoming a professional speaker has become more attractive to business owners, celebrities, and many others." This was eye-opening for me and caused me to rethink my strategy. She went on to share, "So, companies and organizations no longer have to pay these high honorariums as there are a wealth of professional speakers to choose from. As a result, I speak for free, but then I offer my products and programs from the back of the room." The best part of what she shared with me was that she actually makes more money selling from the back of the room than she would get paid from the upfront fee. She later explained that "It must be the right opportunity. There are still some accommodations you'd want the companies or organizations to cover, such as your travel, logistics, and meal expenses."

As I continued my professional development, I would see this back-of-the-room approach followed by speakers, over and over again. It is now called, "selling from the stage." As I attended conferences and workshops, I noticed speakers were offering their products and services from the back of the room. At the end of their presentations, they'd present an offer to the audience to learn more about their topic by attending their other live events, coaching programs, or courses. This prompted me to do some additional research, and what I found astounded me. Only 51% of speakers and entrepreneurs actually made their money receiving an upfront honorarium. In comparison, 49% of speakers made their money by selling their products or services after speaking for free or waiving their fee.

Learning from my research, nearly half, 49% of speakers did not get paid, or paid significantly, to speak. I was DONE! How was it that speakers, myself included, were out there killing themselves to secure a paid speaking opportunity when the speaking legends had figured out how to speak for free and still end up with a paycheck simply by offering their products and services at the end of their presentation? They were capitalizing on the 49% principle.

So, what exactly is this 49% principle? The 49% principle is when a speaker, specifically an entrepreneur who provides a product or service, leverages public speaking as a critical marketing strategy, revenue stream, or income source within their business. This principle disrupts the idea of being paid upfront, to speak. The idea here is, you're giving the audience a taste of who you are and what you do. This introduction is a segway to extend the opportunity to connect with you further. Here you have a chance to build trust and credibility with your audience while also adding value to the overall event.

The audience will begin to decide whether they like you, trust you, resonate with you, or even want to further work with you. This is the value of the 49% principle, and lucrative public speakers are following it every day.

The 49% principle is powerful and, when leveraged correctly, can be an entrepreneur's secret weapon. Let me show you how. Let's say the non-celebrity speaker could potentially earn up to $5,000 per speaking engagement, which isn't bad at all for about an hour-long presentation. However, if you are not getting this type of speaker fee, you can earn this same fee, if not more, by leveraging the 49% principle. Let's say you speak to 100 attendees at an event, in-person or virtually. If you can convert at least 20% of them into buying your $1,000 product, service, or coaching program, you could earn $20,000 (a 20% conversion rate is standard in the speaking industry. Anything higher than that means more money in your pocket). Even if you only convert 10% of your audience into clients, that's still $10,000 you would have earned speaking for free! This model's beauty is you can use this strategy when speaking on other people's stages or create your own stage in the form of a conference, workshop, virtual summit, or masterclass. By adding this strategy to your business model you will potentially have an opportunity for repeat revenue.

Can you see how you can incorporate the 49% principle in your business? Sure, you can get paid upfront to speak, but you can also create your own stage and profit from public speaking without a company or corporation paying you upfront. This is the power of the 49% principle. I want you to take this principle and incorporate it into your business's marketing strategy and plan. My goal is to ensure you are no longer exhausting yourself chasing a speaker fee. Instead, seek meaningful speaking opportunities where you can capitalize on this principle. There is value in your voice—leverage it to build not just a business but a global empire.

There is some science to having a 20% or better customer or client conversion rate. However, my point here is that entrepreneurs have great earning potential when they leverage the 49% principle. Most new speakers and entrepreneurs are still being taught how to secure corporate and other paid speaking engagements. There is nothing wrong with that model. I'm only suggesting diversifying the way you can profit from public speaking as an entrepreneur.

Pitch for Profit

While at Howard University, I entered a public speaking competition called, *Speak Up Speak Off*. The rules of engagement were that each contestant had two minutes to give a motivational speech that experienced speakers would judge. The intention and expectation were that the audience would feel inspired and empowered by the speeches, and the best speaker would win a prize of $1,000.00. The competition was being held, across the country, in California. It took some real hustle on my end to find the funds for a flight to get me there from Washington DC. I recall feeling a little out of my league once I arrived at the venue. Here I was, a young graduate student, standing among some very established individuals, all of whom were there to stake their claim of the cash reward.

This was my very first speaking competition, where I used my voice to win money. We had several opportunities to motivate the audience, and after each round, one speaker was eliminated. At the end of the competition, I was crowned as the winner, and ten crisp $100 bills were placed in my hand.

Kevin Bracy was the host of the competition, and he forever left an impression on me. I felt so full, alive, and accomplished on that stage. As one of the youngest participants, I also felt very confident speaking on stage, and that experience left a lasting impression on me as well. Speaking to compete for cash would eventually be a funding source for my future business ventures.

I share this with you because I want you to explore and be open to the idea of funding your business by leveraging public speaking.

When Purse Paparazzi began to take off, my husband and I quickly realized we needed funding to expand. However, we did not feel comfortable or confident going to a bank and applying for a loan or line of credit. That's when I remembered the speaking and student business pitch competitions at Howard University.

I thought if there were student business pitch competitions, there must be ones for adults too. I hopped on Google and searched for business pitch competitions—looking to use my voice to fund my business.

Most entrepreneurs assume their options are limited to traditional options of securing funding for their business. This is a very inaccurate belief.

So, what is a business pitch competition? A business pitch competition is an opportunity for small business owners to present their business ideas and concepts, in a few seconds or minutes, to a panel of judges and or investors. The judges then decide on the best pitch, and the winner is awarded cash or in-kind prizes. The bonus part of the competition is the benefit of the free publicity and promotion of the participant's businesses. Also with most of the competitions, you don't have to pay the money back.

I want you to know you can fund your business in a non-traditional way. You can get access to capital for your business and start using your voice to pitch for profit. I started entering business pitch competitions on behalf of the Purse Paparazzi and lost more than I won. However, even for the times I lost, the promotion and publicity I received for my business were priceless.

I have won and coached other entrepreneurs to win over $77,000 in funding. I quickly realized that just because you have a great business or idea, that's not enough to succeed. I won competitions because I knew how to speak up for my business and explain what I did in a clear, concise, and compelling way.

I expanded my business by adding a coaching component (yes, another revenue opportunity!). I began coaching entrepreneurs on how to pitch their businesses in competitions and to clients, for profit.

Ebony, one of my first clients, entered her first pitch competition and won a cash prize of $25,000. We worked together to prepare her power pitch, focusing on a crystal-clear message which highlighted her business model, vision, and the overall value she would be providing her customers. We did not leave any room for uncertainty or lack of clarity for the judges. We infused her pitch with high energy and excitement, which left the judges hanging onto her every word. The result? She won!

When it comes to using your voice to generate funds for your business, I want you to be diverse in the funding opportunities you seek. Pitch competitions are a great way to obtain lump sums of cash for your business while sharing your passion for what you do and why you do it. This is what I call pitching for profit. So, your voice, as a black woman, can be used as a funding source in your business. The keys to dominating a pitch competition are:

- **Passion**: Be energized and excited when pitching your business for profit. Your passion for your product or service is contagious. The more fired up you are about it, the more appealing it will be to investors.

- **Funding Ask**: Ask for how much money you need to fund your dreams. Don't hold back. If you need $50,000, don't ask for $20,000. Look at all the costs associated with expanding your business and ask for that amount in your pitch.

- **Twist**: You must be able to show why your product or service is special, unique, or different. This is where you list your competition but show your competitive advantage. Investors love traditional ideas with a twist.

- **Confidence**: Before you open your mouth, investors can tell if you are nervous or not. Nerves aren't bad, but you want to ensure you practice your pitch so you can deliver it with clarity and confidence. Nothing is worse than a great idea with an unconfident person pitching it.

- **How you will use the money**: When asking for investment, be sure to show how you will use the money. Outline if it will be used for inventory, marketing, or human resources (to name a few ways). This shows investors you have planned on how you will use their investment. It makes them confident knowing you will execute the plan once the investment is secured.

Giving an exciting business pitch takes some planning and creativity. This will go a long way, especially when you are up against traditional investors, angel investors, or venture capitalists. You must master the opening of your pitch. The first few seconds should be a hook or grab the attention of those who are listening. Once you have their attention, you must keep them hooked. You need to get to your point quickly while not sounding rushed or unsure. The craft here is finding the perfect harmony between being clear, concise, and compelling.

You must infuse your pitch with enthusiasm, energy, and excitement. This is not merely having the 'right words'; it means so much more. Your body language, including eye contact and tonality, is critical in exhibiting the passion and love you have for your business. No one wants to listen to a monotone, bulleted list of your business, no matter how great it may be. They are more interested in being excited about your business, the profit potential, and how well you can explain it, which helps drive their investment decisions. Now, I am not talking about excitement for the sake of exhibiting excitement. Investors and judges are looking for sincere and genuine passion from you. They are not looking to be entertained by your enthusiasm. While you may have a dynamic product or service, they are looking for you to be excited and enthused because you know what you offer is so good that they will not want to miss out, which will get them to fund your business venture.

I was focused and used my voice to fund my business and taught others how to do the same. My mind was set on funding my business through pitch competitions, and I did just that. Here is the good news, you can too!

By speaking up for your business, you can use public speaking and pitching as a funding source in your business. Investors are always interested in innovative ideas. Whenever you pitch for your business, and especially if you are pitching for money, you must include very clear and specific points highlighting the uniqueness and innovation in your product or service. I think it is essential for me to give this fair warning; you do not want to be so unique that it provides the sense that you have a one-and-done product or service. Investors are keenly interested in products and services that have long-term revenue potential. My point here is, do not box yourself in either. Finding the right balance between a traditional idea with your unique twist is what sells. Being too complicated will confuse your audience.

A winning pitch must always be clear and transparent about what type of investment you hope to gain access to and how you will put those funds to use. Investors want to know key points about your business, and you should be prepared to include these in your pitch. Do not forget! This needs to be done clearly and concisely, as each element of your pitch should be. When trying to compact a power punch of passion, innovation, enthusiasm, and your specific investment request, it's a delicate balancing act to ask into one strategic message. None of these elements should be considered less important than the other, especially not your specific investment request. Investors may love what you are saying and may be interested in partnering with you, but without knowing how much funding your need and how it will be used, they are left in the abyss of ambiguity, and that alone can cost you the money you sought after. Most of us play it safe. I urge you not to. Be bold and audacious in your asking. Investors do not want to open their wallets to timid business ventures. Investors are interested in ambitious and assertive entrepreneurs and businesses they can believe in and standby. So, whatever you need for your business, ask for it!

Whether you are attempting your first or tenth pitch competition, you need to be thoroughly prepared. Master, knowing your business, your consumers, the value your business carries, and its vitality for long-term success. Black women, I want you to exude confidence in who you are, what you provide, and how you serve. We are the backbone of small businesses. You may find yourself in a room full of people who do not look like you. You may also find yourself pitching to judges who do not look like you. But neither of these situations should impede you from pressing ahead and including pitch competitions as part of your business funding generation strategy.

It is crucial to include pitching as a vital part of your funding model. Only 2% of women receive the funding they need for their businesses. And while black women are the most extensive and fastest-growing group of small business owners and startups, of that same 2%, they make-up only .06% of business owners who receive the money they need for their businesses. For these reasons and so many more, I repeat, you must pivot your business strategy to include pitching for profit.

Turn Conversations
Into Cash

There are the necessities we need to ensure we legitimize our businesses. There are also the necessary things we must invest in so that our companies are operational. However, our lists are often void of planning on answering one simple question, "What do you do?" Our answer to that question represents the backbone of our business. I believe, if you can answer this question clearly, confidently, and concisely, it will lead to revenue for your business.

If an entrepreneur can command a conversation in a manner that highlights the value they offer and the benefits to their clients and consumers, they can turn conversations into cash. And we know cash is 'queen' in business. The challenge that exists is that black-women entrepreneurs don't have the know-how to have cash-churning conversations, whether in-person or virtually. It is instrumental to your business's success in learning how to have conversations that lead to cash.

If you want to master the art of turning conversations into cash, you will need a verbal business card. A verbal business card has four requirements. Each requirement is crucial to it's effectiveness.

1. Clear, concise, and compelling. Your message should be music to the ears of your audience. Here is not the time for ambiguity. It would be best if you spoke

directly to your audience in a way that begins to lead them towards deciding to invest in your product, program, or service.

2. Focus on psychographics over demographics. Here is where you specifically zoom in on your target client or customer. A demographic focus does not equate to a conversion. Thinking only about how much money your client earns, whether or not they own a home, have a car, their education levels, etc., may limit your ability to reach your audience. For example, a six-figure earner may be able to afford your product or service on paper, but they live outside of their means and cannot allocate funds to invest. However, when you focus on your target client or customers' psychographics, it makes a world of difference. You will zero in on what they care about, their values, what gives them pleasure or causes them pain. When you tap into these areas, you invoke emotion in your audience, and it is from that emotional place, they will make their buying or investment decision.

3. Being clear on who you serve. This is

somewhat of a personal reflection. I serve black women entrepreneurs, who are also speakers. The reason I focus on this audience is that I have a personal affinity with them. In a sense, I am serving myself. You must understand your target audience, their challenges, what keeps them up at night, their desires, and more.

4. Use 'luxury language' and avoid 'discount dialect.' 'Luxury language' are words and phrases that speak to the greatness of your business. This language highlights what you do and how you serve securely. Words like transform, encourage, empower, and equip are luxurious words that value your greatness and the greatness your clients will walk away with after working with you. 'Discount dialect' are words that devalue what you do, who you are, and how you serve your clients or customers. Terms that fall within this category are, "help," "all I do," or "I just do this." I want you to avoid these words and terms at all costs. They leave your audience with a sense of mediocrity in your brand, your service, or your product. They take away from

your greatness. Do not disrespect your worth, your hard work, your knowledge, or your skills. Your experience, expertise, knowledge, failures, successes, and client testimonies are all a part of your success story, which deserves language that elevates who you are and what you do. And you certainly do more than just help people.

Now that you understand the framework for a verbal business card, I encourage you to assess how you have been talking about your business, products, or services. Take a hard look, my fellow black-women business owners and speakers, and be honest with yourselves so that you can begin to elevate your business and open yourself up to increased success.

Let's get your verbal business card done so that you may start to turn your conversations into cash.

10

Power at
the Podium

If you want to profit from public speaking, there is a three-prong approach you must master. This formula will teach you how to speak for profit on and offline. This trifecta will prove crucial for your speaking success, 1) having a verbal business card, 2) master your power presentation, and 3) communicate to convert. Once you have all three of these factors covered, you will be well on your way to profit from the use of your voice.

Your verbal business card is the foundation of your ability to articulate what you do, how you serve, and the outcome your clients may expect after working with you. In essence, your verbal business card is your elevator pitch on steroids. You can tell the world and your target client what you do in a way that's clear, concise, and compelling.

Most people, nowadays, have a short attention span. We are inundated with information like never before. Technology has made it easy for us to find what we want with just the click of a button. Additionally, with the increased volume of video traffic on social media, the users focus has been split a thousand ways. Therefore, you have a small window of opportunity to grab and hold the viewers' attention. Here is where your verbal business card is crucial. It allows you to capture the attention of your audience quickly.

If people are bored, they won't buy. You must avoid being content-rich but delivery poor. This means you have to polish your presentation and sharpen your speaking skills as an entrepreneur who will profit from public speaking. You must speak with power at the podium, which includes more than just being a good speaker. You want to be energetic and magnetic. You also want to persuade your audience to pay you after your presentation while positioning yourself as an authority on your topic. This is when credibility happens, and the more conversations you have with prospects can lead to cash. Essentially speaking with power at the podium all boils down to how you can effectively communicate to convert.

Many paid speakers will tell you that you should have a go-to signature talk. A signature talk is an essential asset for a speaker in the speaking industry. Typically, professional speakers who are paid an upfront honorarium are always prepared to speak because they have their go-to signature talk. This talk is usually 30-90 minutes of valuable content, which event hosts and planners are willing to pay for them to share with their audiences. Having a signature talk is perfect for speakers and entrepreneurs who are consistently getting paid upfront to speak.

However, if you do not have a signature talk, you still have many opportunities to profit from speaking by leveraging your power presentation. Your power presentation encourages people to buy your product or service or enroll in your coaching program instantly after you speak. This is using the 49% principle to your advantage. The goal of speaking with power at the podium is to communicate to convert, so the entire audience becomes your potential client.

Yes, you want to motivate, inspire, and empower your audience, but you also want to persuade them to buy into whatever you are offering at the end of your presentation. You can do that with a power presentation and speaking with power at the podium.

So, what does it mean when you are communicating to convert? Communicating to convert is when you deliver a presentation, virtually or in-person, intending to get your audience to take action with you after you speak. Ultimately, even if no one is paying you upfront to speak, you create an opportunity to be profitable.

The keys to unlocking your power at the podium are

clarity in your message, confidence in your delivery, and having an offer at the end of your presentation. The more confident you are with your product, program, or service offer, the easier it is for your audience to convert into paying clients.

The introduction of your power presentation should not be boring or a slow build-up. Your introduction should be attention-grabbing and crafted to 'hook' your audience as soon as you open your mouth. Your voice should be able to penetrate the ears of everyone listening virtually or in-person. If your goal is to communicate to convert, you must speak with energy, enthusiasm, excitement, confidence, and clarity to grab and hold their attention. You are competing with text messaging, social media, and many other distractions, so grabbing their attention is crucial when speaking with power at the podium.

(TIP) **Attention-grabbing techniques that will give you *Power at the Podium:***

- Have a hook or attention snatching line in your opening.
- Open your presentation with a story.
- Share a startling statistic or fact.
- Challenge a train of thought.

- Ask a thought-provoking question.

Power Presentation

1. **Hook.** Grab the audience's attention with a joke, story, fact, or startling statistic.

2. **Verbal Business Card.** A clear, concise, and compelling way to answer the questions what do you "DO" with confidence that takes people from interested to invested in working with you after just one conversation

3. **Belief Statement.** Your belief statement is your unique perspective and beliefs on your topic.

4. **Tell a story.** Make your first point by telling a story that connects to your offer.

5. **Drop a seed.** A seed is a hint about what you will offer.

6. **Demonstrate expertise.** Make your second point by teaching your audience something they did not already know or cannot easily

find through a Google search. Demonstrate your expertise on your topic.

7. **Drop another seed.** Offer the opportunity for your audience to work with you beyond your presentation.

8. **Show your receipts.** Here is where you can take people from interested to invested. Showcase your successes by sharing stories of past and current clients. Talk about where they were before working with you and where they landed after working with you. If you are just starting in your business and do not have any success stories to showcase, focus on highlighting how you have benefited from your idea or philosophy, which has been the driving factor for your business.

9. **Make your offer/end with your Call-To-Action.** What you want the audience to do instantly after hearing you speak.

Follow these tips, and you are well on your way to leveraging your voice and public speaking as a lead generation tool to sell your product, service, or coaching program as an entrepreneur who speaks.

This is the bread and butter of how I teach my coaching clients to profit from public speaking even if no one is paying them upfront.

Create Your Stage

Now that I have taught you the strategies needed to profit from public speaking, I want to take you to the next level. It's now time to create your stage.

You don't have to wait for an invite to profit from public speaking. Start with being proactive in identifying, pursuing, and creating your own speaking opportunities. When you are proactive, you control your speaking journey and control when and how you get paid as a black woman in business. You get to decide on the types of events you are interested in speaking at and even how you want to speak, virtually, in-person, live, recorded, or on someone else's platform. Or you can speak on a platform entirely created by you. My recommendation is to select at least 2-3 stages to speak on and dominate.

Another critical component for creating your stage is to decide what type of speaker you really are. Understand that no one is tied to being just one type of speaker. Most often, speakers are a combination of at least two speaker types. Understanding and owning the kind of speaker you are will contribute to your confidence and ultimately help you profit from public speaking.

Five types of Speakers

Let's dive into the five different types of speakers.

1. **Motivational Speaker** - is one of the most common speaker types used in the industry. I find that this speaker type is overused because speakers are unaware of the other speaker types. Nonetheless, the motivational speaker is exceptional at energizing and motivating their audiences. They are a refreshing reminder to dream big, go after your goals, and make their audiences believe the impossible is possible. While everyone isn't a motivational speaker, every presentation or speech should have some motivation in it. Some notable motivational speakers are Les Brown and Eric Thomas.

2. **Transformational Speaker** - is a type of speaker aiming to create some transformation for their audience. People typically seek transformational speakers because they are dealing with a specific experience or situation and are looking to come out refreshed, renewed, or reset on a new trajectory or course in life, their career, or business.

Transformational speakers have somewhat of a responsibility to heal or make-whole, or set-free, their audiences. An example of a terrific transformational speaker is Lisa Nichols.

3. **Spiritual Speaker** - A spiritual speaker is generally associated with being in a ministry, religious group, or organization. They often speak from a pulpit, but that is not a requirement. However, spiritual speakers usually deliver faith-based messages and share their beliefs about God or another higher power they may believe in. Reading scripture and or encouraging prayer constitutes a significant part of the spiritual speakers' assets and content. The individual whose speaker type is spiritual maintains an aura or demeanor of authority, and they use terms and words that are religious. Notable spiritual speakers are Bishop T.D. Jakes and Joyce Meyer.

4. **Informational Speaker** - An informative speaker delivers just that, information. I admit this may not be my favorite type of speaker. I feel like they are content-rich and delivery poor. They have excellent and extremely

valuable content, yet they may be a bit stoic or rigid when delivering their messages. These are matter-of-fact speakers. They aren't necessarily interested in motivating audiences. They are more interested in educating, sharing data, statistical information, or quantitative analyses. In my experience, they are professors, researchers, and private businesspeople. You may find informational speakers at academic or research conferences. Please make no mistake, informative speakers are paid handsomely to speak and share their information, and they have a substantial audience.

5. **Inspirational Speaker** - This is the speaker who typically has a life story that is like no other. They have endured and overcome significant adversity, challenges, or obstacles. The inspirational speaker gives hope to those who may have lost hope in their situations. The audiences they serve are very diverse; in thought, race, gender, financial, and social classes, and that's how they reach them through their messages.

Inspirational speakers are unforgettable. Their stories stick with the listener and often leave a lasting impression. This type of speaker is captivating and generally has their audience hanging on their every word. They invoke compassion, empathy, and togetherness within anyone who hears them talk. Some dynamic, inspirational speakers are Oprah Winfrey and Michelle Obama.

The more you understand the kind of speaker you are, the better stage you can select to speak and serve. You want to be sure there's alignment between your message, your audience, and your offer. In doing so, this will undoubtedly contribute to your elevation as a speaker.

TIP **The assets and intellectual property you need to create your stage:**

- **Branded marketing materials.** Items that will market and promote you as a speaker including your headshot, one sheet, Electronic Press Kit, action photos, services and speaking reel.

- **Bold Biography.** This is not a generic bio that gives a rundown of your resume and expression of love for your family. Your Bio should be bold and speak directly to your accomplishments and experiences. This is not the time to be timid or humble. Here is your opportunity to "toot your own horn" for a change.

- **Professional headshot.** This also does not have to be bland, stoic, and boring. Be on brand, show some personality, engage with your audience through your picture. But beware, this is for professional use. DO NOT use a 'selfie' as your headshot.

- **Electronic Press Kit (EPK).** This is a branded one-sheet, which highlights your accomplishments in a more concise way. It's used to highlight your expertise and allows you to name-drop all the 'stages' you've graced. As this is a visual tool, you will need the logos of the engagements where you have spoken. The EPK includes:

    ○ Your Biography.

- o Your speaking topics.
- o Testimonials.
- o Action shots. These are shots of you delivering your message, including photos of your audience.
- o Media coverage.
- o Links and instructions on how to 'book' you for speaking engagements.

- **A professionally and well-branded website.** Be sure your website has a page dedicated to showcasing you as a speaker.

Speaking on
Social Stages

Social media is a great way to broadcast your brilliance. It is a terrific way to build an online tribe and community. Social media can create connections and relationships with your target client that can attract them to your business. As a speaker and entrepreneur, your brand strategy should include speaking and building a substantial social media presence.

There are many social media outlets, and they all can serve a specific purpose for you and your business. Speaking on these social stages has several benefits and opportunities. One of the most incredible opportunities of social media is to build your organic audience. You can build a following who sincerely trusts and believes in your platform by simply showing up consistently and continuously. However, do not underestimate the "simple" part. There is quite a bit of work on your part. Not only will you need to show up regularly, but you must also provide quality information and value that serves the needs and wants of your followers.

There's something to be said about the person who shows up on social media professionally, authentically, and consistently. Their audience supports them and become very loyal followers for life.

Speaking on social stages can also open doors for in-person and other virtual speaking opportunities. Event holders seeking speakers for their events often assess your audience engagement to determine if having your name on their event will draw attendees. If you have a robust social speaking presence, this could earn you a spot on other stages.

A solid fan base on social media can have a positive financial impact on your business. This is undoubtedly a benefit of building your social media presence.

Good written content and beautiful imagery are not enough. Inspirational quotes and motivational messages are tremendous and certainly needed at times. However, these do not necessarily convert a follower into a consumer. Consumers are savvy and want to know who they are spending their money with. Using your voice on social stages gives you an opportunity, and in some instances, an advantage in your business, as you can connect with your audience in a way that static content does not allow.

Your level of engagement with your follower base demonstrates your commitment to serving them. When you provide quality information, insight, guidance, and tips that help them in their endeavors or meet their immediate and or long-term needs, it opens doors for you to convert them to consumers.

(TIP) **How to Speak on Social Stages:**

- **Be consistent and show up regularly.** Ideally, showing up at regular intervals (same day and same time) helps your audience plan their participation. This is your Prime Time! I'm reminded of something I heard, and that has stuck with me, "visibility trumps ability any day."

- **Share quality content that ties directly to your business and brand.** One thing I find beneficial is to provide content or tips using a numbered list of points. Examples are:
  - Three ways to...
  - Six tips on how to...
  - Five steps for...
  - The number one thing holding you back in business...

- **Pick one platform and dominate it before moving to another.** I have seen many instances where speakers and entrepreneurs get caught up trying to master all social media platforms at once. My guidance would be to identify where you have the most engagement from your audience and "Go-Hard," showing up for them. Once you have solidified your presence on one platform, then strategically add the others, one at a time.

- **Be sure your graphics are clear and visually stimulating.** Part of your online presence is the visual effects that align with your brand. I would recommend having these done professionally. However, if you have budgetary constraints, try other, less expensive platforms (i.e., Canva).

- **Always have a Call-to-Action (CTA).** You should have a variety of CTA's to use at the appropriate time and for the right audience. Examples of

CTA's are: Follow me [on my social media platforms], subscribe to my [YouTube Page], sign-up to receive [my quarterly newsletter], etc.

- **Use your verbal business card.** There is nothing worse than someone joining your 'live' video, listening to your talking points, yet they don't know who you are, what you do, and how you can serve them. So, I suggest, as you're speaking, you should be sure to communicate your business to your audience multiple times throughout your 'live.' This may mean you give your credentials at the beginning, middle, and end of your video, at a minimum. Suggested questions to ask yourself are, "Am I providing people a way to work with me after listening to my presentation?" and "Am I telling them exactly how to do that?"

Listed below are some of the top social stages to attract and convert clients. Select one or two and dominate. Trying to be on all of them won't work and will leave you burned out. Choose the platforms your clients or customer spend the most time on so you can easily connect with them.

Below are several social media platforms where you can make your voice visible and attract more clients to your business.

- Facebook [Live]
- Instagram [LIVE or Stories]
- LinkedIn [Live or Video]
- Podcast
- YouTube
- TikTok
- Snapchat
- Clubhouse

Speak to Serve

If you want to profit from public speaking or turn conversations into cash, one of the things you must master is the ability to speak and serve. Speaking and serving are categorically different than speaking to sell. There is a massive craze in the speaking industry where speakers focus on using the stage to pitch their products and services and spend less time serving their audiences. I refer to this trend as "product puking." The messages are nauseating because the speaker's or presenter's focus is to sell only and not provide value or solutions to the audience.

The get-rich-quick schemes may have worked for a while, but event planners have realized that their intention to invite speakers to speak and serve their audiences has somehow turned into a big sales pitch or gimmick. This is why I want you to be responsible when using your voice to serve others.

I pride myself on speaking to serve my audiences. I have adopted this philosophy. When I grace the stage, I intend to show the audience how my product or services can enhance their lives or transform their businesses. I encourage you to begin speaking to serve by adding value to your audiences. The most expensive thing someone can pay you is their attention. You want to make the time you have with your audience valuable by offering them tips, tricks, and transformations they can use right away to elevate their business or life.

Once you adopt this philosophy, you will find a more engaged audience who finds value in your message. You will begin to build trust and credibility with your audience. The result will be increased conversions and sales.

Before we go any further on this topic, I want to take a moment to talk about what I call "discount dialect." Discount dialect reduces the impact of your message and can turn your audience away. It doesn't serve. It sells. It doesn't empower. It discourages. It doesn't add value. It makes your audience feel like an ATM. The word *sell* is an example of discount dialect. People don't like to feel like they are always being sold something and not receiving any value when they hear speakers speak. There is a fine line between selling and serving. If you want to profit from public speaking, you must put serving before selling.

Consumers have also become very savvy and can sniff out the desperation in sellers. However, if you present your product or service in a beneficial way to your audience, they will be more open to investing in what you're offering. So, the first thing I want you to do is to have the audience in mind. Ask yourself, "How am I going to serve my audience? How am I going to add value to their experience of hearing me speak?" It is all about the audience when you're speaking. You are speaking to motivate, inspire, impact, persuade, and then offer your product or service.

To truly serve your audience, you must first know your audience. One of the biggest mistakes novice speakers make is they agree to speak on stages where no one is in their target audiences. You want to be sure that you understand the platform you'll be speaking on and have insight into the audience the event will bring in. Are they in your target market? Will your message be of value to them? Have your audience in mind and understand a little bit about who they are. And yes, this may mean passing on opportunities to speak on stages where there isn't anyone in your target market. Make defining your audience a priority. Once you define them, you'll be clear on who your audience is, and this will help you determine where you should be speaking and serving.

I speak to black women in business. Can I talk to Asian women, Latina women, or white women in business? Absolutely. However, my target market is black women in business. Why? Because I can resonate with their voices, experiences, and expectations. Therefore, as I created my talk, I had this audience in mind. I serve them through exciting talking points and my speaking style. I use analogies, terms, and stories they can relate to.

Knowing who my audience is, having them in mind when I prepare my talk, and resonating with them by sharing a message that adds value helps me build trust, credibility, and likeability. Then, and only then, will I offer my products and services.

14

Pimp Your Passion

We have all heard the saying, "multiple streams of income." The concept of having multiple streams of income intends for people to optimize a variety of means for generating income and not just depending on one job. However, as many women have begun pursuing their endeavors of having multiple streams of income, the concept seems to have become entirely misconstrued. Now, don't get me wrong, I'm an advocate and proponent for having multiple income streams. The issue I have is some people have confused the idea of multiple income streams with doing a bunch of different things to earn money instead of employing strategies that result in long-term income and wealth. As a speaker and an entrepreneur, I encourage you not to fall victim to the misconception of what it means to have multiple streams of income. Here I want to introduce you to another concept. One that can lead you to create long-term sustainability for your business, revenue, and wealth. What I am talking about here is what I call "Pimp Your Passion."

So, what do I mean when I say, "Pimp Your Passion?" I mean, identify what you are passionate about and the multiple ways you can get paid for doing what you already love. Pimping your passion and various streams of income are not synonymous. They are distinctly different. When you have multiple income streams, it is like wearing multiple 'hats' or playing various roles. For example, you may be a Sales Representative for Mary Kaye, a stock trader, a real estate broker, and have your own small business as a tax advisor. All these roles make up your portfolio of multiple streams of income. However, none, or at least, not all, are your true passion. Furthermore, each role requires you to divide your time, attention, and skills, pulling you in many different directions.

When you pimp your passion, it allows you to find a common core of skill and desire, treat them as the nucleus and build your income streams around them. I'll use myself as a living example. Speaking is the nucleus of who I am and what I am passionate about doing. Therefore, I have built multiple streams of income around my love for speaking. I am paid for speaking on other people's stages, I am paid for speaking and teaching speaking through seminars, workshops, and course structures, and I've created an entire speaking business and brand, all centered around my passion. I even wrote this book, which is another revenue stream directly tied to my passion. As you can see, I have multiple streams of income by merely pimping my passion.

When you pimp your passion, you are taking what

you love, are good at, passionate about, and turning it into the core of your prongs of income. As a speaker and entrepreneur, I want you to see the value of using what you are already passionate about. I want you to create a plan and strategy that will ensure you generate a combination of income lanes and create a lifestyle full of joy because you are loving what you do and doing what you love.

In case I haven't convinced you to rethink and re-strategize your approach by considering pimping your passion, I'll give you another example. Let's take a look at Beyonce. Beyonce is the epitome of how to pimp your passion. At her core, she is an entertainer. She sings, dances, and performs; that's her nucleus. She has built an entire empire around her passion. She has pimped it to the max. She receives income in various ways, including concerts, royalties from music sales, movies, endorsements, and apparel, to name a few. Notice that none of these are outside of her bullseye. By creating her income streams centered around her passion, Beyonce has positioned herself to stay focused on doing what she loves and building long-term income and wealth by pimping her passion.

So, as a speaker and entrepreneur, I encourage you not to focus on merely having multiple income streams but instead focus on pimping your passion.

Speaking with Style

93% of communication is nonverbal. So, that means as a speaker, you are communicating with more than just your words. You are communicating with your body, your eyes, your hands, and even your wardrobe. These non-verbal cues give your audience some insight as to who you are. They may begin to formulate opinions about you based on these non-verbal cues. Therefore, if you truly want to profit from public speaking, you need to focus on your overall presence, which makes up your authentic speaking style. What you are not saying is just as important as what you are saying.

I want to dive into how you can find your authentic speaking style and focus on what that means for you as a speaker. When speaking in front of an audience, live or virtually, you want to be sure your non-verbal cues are aligned with what you say. Your body language sends clear messages to your audience on your level of engagement with them. Your posture, they way you are sitting, folded arms, and even the way you are standing, can all indicate your lack of interest, motivation, and energy. And this, in turn, is reciprocated by your audience.

Additionally, the way you dress is just as important. If you show up messy and sloppy, your audience is less likely to trust what you are saying; you may be the Albert Einstein on your topic, but they will not hear you. This is also applies to your hair, make-up, and so on. Being authentic yet mindful of your overall verbal and non-verbal cues will go a long way with your audience and help your business.

During a presentation I was delivering, about 30-minutes in, my feet began to hurt, in my heels. I was in so much pain that I could feel myself crouching down to find relief. At this point, my focus was on my aching feet. All I could think about was getting out of my shoes and into some comfortable sneakers. My non-verbal cues conveyed that I was distracted by something. This was a valuable lesson because I realized that I could not effectively serve and attend to my audience if my feet were competing for my attention. So, I knew I needed to make a drastic change and get more authentic in my speaking style; a style that afforded me the physical comfort I needed to sustain while on the stage, as well as a cute and chic style that represented my personality. So, I began speaking in my sneakers, what I call "speak in sneaks." Wearing my sneakers while I spoke resonated with my authentic speaking and personal style, while giving me comfort. I needed to go the long-haul when speaking while staying completely focused and engaged with my audience.

There is no hard and fast rule about a woman wearing heels and a business suit to speak on any platform. Of course, you must know the culture of the company or event you're speaking at. However, when you show up as your authentic self and execute in your authentic speaking style, you have a much greater chance of genuinely connecting with your audience. Therefore, ask yourself, "What is my authentic speaking style?" Know it. And own it.

Another thing to consider when getting in tune with your authentic speaking style is whether you prefer to use props when speaking. A great example of this is the hand-held mic versus the lavalier. Do you prefer a hand-held mic that allows you to easily roam the stage? A podium where you are stationary? Or, a lavalier, where you have greater flexibility to walk around the stage or even perhaps into the audience? These are all things to think about when determining who you are, authentically, as a speaker. Now, do not make these decisions without considering all elements. You may think you prefer to speak at a podium, when in fact, if you're like me, very animated when you speak, your speaking style may call for a lavalier. In this case, a podium may clash with your speaking style.

Remember, always be authentic and keep an eye out for those verbal and non-verbal cues. Find what works for YOU! Don't try and copy someone else's style or alter what makes you comfortable because you're worried about how you'll be received. Stay true to your authentic speaking style because your audience, the right audience for you, will appreciate you all the more for it. You'll have more influence, credibility, and connection when you are authentic. And that authenticity may turn into revenue for your business.

Speak Up Black Women!

As a black woman entrepreneur, I repeat, leveraging your voice as a lead generation tool, your business's marketing strategy and revenue stream are non-negotiable. My goal in writing this book is for you to understand that you don't have to be a great speaker to communicate to convert. I want you to embrace your voice and view it as your secret weapon in business that makes you special, different, and unique.

If you desire to increase your income and influence as a disruptor in your industry, it's time to speak up!

Now that you are at the end of this book but at the beginning of a perspective change as an entrepreneur who speaks, I want you to pick one of the concepts covered to leverage your voice in your business and run with it. Too often, we read books, get overwhelmed with information, and do nothing. I don't want that to be you. Look at all the ways I mentioned to boost your business so you can profit from public speaking.

Getting focused on how you will use your voice will give you the confidence and clarity to move forward. I recommend the Verbal Business Card to start. It's how people first connect and relate to you.

Answering the questions, "What do you do?" or

"What do you speak about?" is the foundation for profiting from public speaking. You want to master the art of being the spokesperson for your business, book, or brand, so your voice becomes your #1 marketing strategy.

The time of you playing it safe or settling in your business has expired. Now that you have this book in your hands, you have a mandate to open your mouth and attract money and opportunities in a way that will rock your world and blow your mind. We have all heard the phrase "A closed mouth doesn't get fed." and that's 100% true in business.

I'm grateful that you've stuck with me. It means you know, understand, and accept the value in your voice. If you are still trying to put your Verbal Business Card pieces together, feel free to connect with me. My superpower is making your voice visible by showing you how to be an advocate for your awesomeness so you can verbalize your value in a way that's clear, concise, and compelling.

Verbal Business Card In Action

Pitch before VBC

Verbal Business Card

I'm a mental health counselor

I SHATTER misconceptions for women who STRUGGLE saying NO! I show them how to make self-care non-negotiable by infusing BOUNDARIES in their lives, so they transition from voiceless to VOCAL in their personal and professional relationships.

Pitch before VBC

Verbal Business Card

I'm a photographer

I CAPTURE the legacy of families, so they have memorable photos that last a LIFETIME!

Pitch before VBC

Verbal Business Card

I'm a virtual assistant

I CREATE systems and structures for entrepreneurs with a BIG vision. I handle the details of their business so they can operate in their calling worry-free!

 LUXURY LANGUAGE POWER WORDS

You are one step closer to Turning Conversations into Cash and making a PROFIT from Public Speaking!

Check out these **power** words that will give your business or brand message an INSTANT makeover.

Remember to use Luxury Language and NOT Discount Dialect when telling potential clients what you "DO" or speak about.

Luxury Language Power Words

Advance	Create	Disrupt	Provide
Advocate	Deliver	Educate	Recover
Alter	Demolish	Eliminate	Reduce
Assist	Design	Empower	Replenish
Challenge	Develop	Improve	Teach
Champion	Discover	Increase	Transform

Why I wrote *Speak Black Woman*

Have you begun receiving requests to participate as a guest speaker or panelist at various conferences, events, and summits? Yet, none of these opportunities are paid? Are you wasting hours filling out speaker proposals and not getting selected? Are you stuck trying to figure out how you can still profit from public speaking as the host of your own virtual or in-person events? Or maybe you are trying to leverage your voice on social media, hosting a Masterclass or multi-day challenge, yet your communication on these platforms fails to convert?

I want you to know you are not alone. Many women in business who are passionate about public speaking are having challenges monetizing their message. This is precisely why I wrote this book. I am here to ensure you never have to wonder how you can profit from public speaking again!

No more being tired of wasting time speaking and walking away feeling undervalued or underappreciated by the audience or event organizer. *Speak Black Woman* teaches you how to strategically leverage public speaking in your business as a lead generation and marketing strategy. You will find some "Q-Tips" that will prove to be kick-starters to leveraging your voice for your business.

You may have become a speaker by accident, o maybe you willingly raised your hand to speak and serve audiences with your message and your mess either way, if you want to make money as a speaker *Speak Black Woman* was created to help you do jus that.

In this book, I have taught you how to use you voice and message to reach your audience by the masses and reduce the one-on-one model so tha you can take your life, sanity, and time back. Onc you learn and apply these speaking strategies, you'l appreciate getting back the luxury of being presen for your family and having harmony between you home life and your business.

The lessons and strategies in *Speak Black Woman* are not meant to compete or replace your revenue model for securing upfront fees to speak. It is intended to complement your marketing strategies and to maximize and monetize speaking opportunities to attract loyal clients and customers ready to do business with you for life.

This book is focused on black women with service-based businesses. If you want to offer a coaching program, online course, host virtual events, or some other professional service and want to invite people to work with you, instantly after speaking, *Speak Black Woman* has your name written all over it.

So, sit back, enjoy the journey to profit from public speaking. **Speak, black woman!**

About the Author

Quinn Conyers

Quinn Conyers broadcasts the brilliance in black women's voices in business by training them how to turn conversations into cash so they can profit from public speaking, virtually and in person.

Quinn believes public speaking is the number one marketing strategy every woman in business must master to be successful. She trains women on how to leverage public speaking as a marketing strategy, lead generator, and revenue stream within their business. Her goal is to empower women to maximize and monetize all speaking opportunities on behalf of their business, book, or brand, even if no one pays them an upfront speaker's fee.

With over 14-years of speaking, training, and sales experience, Quinn takes pride in giving female business owners a messaging makeover. She is dynamic in transforming entrepreneurs from public speakers into power presenters. She is also gifted in upgrading boring and basic elevator pitches into a clear, concise, and compelling verbal business card.

As an energetic event emcee and powerful presenter, Quinn brings a unique flair to elevating boring events into epic experiences. Quinn has made her voice visible on many virtual and in-person stages. Some of her most notable speaking opportunities are the MPT Women's Leadership Forum, the National Black MBA Association, National Association of Women Business Owners (NAWBO), E-Women's Network, the Women's Business Center of Charlotte, Black Speakers Network (BSN), Better Business Bureau (BBB), and Essence Magazine Young Women's Leadership Conference.

As a result of Quinn's accomplishments, she has been featured in *Black Enterprise, Essence,*

Speakers, *So Empowered Young Money*, and a host of local magazines and newspapers in DC, Maryland, and Virginia. She has also graced the covers of *Vision and Purpose* and *Empowering Women to Speak Out* magazines.

Quinn is a pitch master and has made it to the 2nd round of Shark Tank auditions four times. She has also appeared on the Entrepreneurs Elevator Pitch TV Show and has won $77,000, pitching her business in various pitch competitions.

Teaching others is a passion of Quinn's, and she incorporates learning into all aspects of her business and speaking. She is the Speak Black Woman podcast host and sits on the Global Black Women Chamber of Commerce (GBWCC) board and the Better Business Bureau (BBB). She's a former professor of Speech Communications at Coppin State University and is currently a faculty member at Black Speakers University (BSU). Quinn has also authored two books.

Quinn is originally from Lancaster, Pennsylvania but now resides in Baltimore, Maryland, with her husband and two sons. She earned her Bachelor's degree from West Chester University and a Master's degree from Howard University.

Quinn's ultimate goal is to speak at the annual

Essence Fest hosted by Essence Magazine. She would also love to host a nationally broadcasted awards show that highlights black people's achievements. Her long-term vision is to executive produce her own reality TV-based competition for African American men and women who desire to be motivational speakers.

WORK WITH QUINN

To Book Quinn as a Speaker, Trainer or Coach visit:
www.QuinnConyers.com

To be a part of the Speak Black Women Movement
visit: www.SpeakBlackWoman.com